Confessions of a Teenage Mind
By: Makayla Camille

Cover Illustrations by: Sarah Joy and Lia Frenae

INTRODUCTION

I was born with the idea that *anything is possible*. If I try hard enough, I can accomplish anything that I set my mind to. I can control the world around me and what I give to it and what I take away from it. That idea has stayed with me all throughout my life. Because of that little saying that, *anything is possible* and this is just a little piece of what runs through my teenage mind. With the concepts of love, friendship, politics, mental health, being a woman, race, family, art, faith and then just life in general. This book of poetry is one passion of mine and I hope this shows the confessions of my teenage mind.

Always Yours,
MCB

P.S
I hope you enjoy my book; it's short and sweet like me.

Table of Contents

Love
Friendship
Politics
Mental Health
I Am Women
Race
Family
Art
Life

LOVE

What is Love?
Is it a bond that cannot be broken?
Or just an element that makes you human?
That is a question only you can answer

Untitled

My lips bleed when you kiss me with thorn lips
You say we are perfect when you know we don't fit
I should call you love but the words never seem to escape
This is the path I do not want to take
Because this love is not fate

Lost

I gave him my love
But he let someone else take his
If he really was mine
His love would not have been taken so easily
I guess you can say I loved and I lost

Love

Love lies
Love kills
Love wins
Love heals
Love grows
Love helps
Love blooms
Love enables
Love explains
Love destroys
Love understands
And love will never end

Untitled

Love is like dying
Because you don't know if
You're going to end up with hell
Or Heaven
But it's a risk worth taking

Love Lies

Love is not in your kiss
Or the way you move your hips
It's how you hold me when I am low
When I don't know where I belong
And you make me feel like I am at home
When I can see a better version of myself
Every time I look into your big eyes
That's how I know where your love lies

"I hate you..."
No you don't
You love me

FRIENDSHIP

Dear. Friend
Let's make some life long memories

My Dear Friend

My dear friend
I love you so
You are amazing in every single way
I am so happy that I met you
Because you are the brightest part of my day

Untitled

You might lose a friend
You might gain a friend
But in the end
Enjoy it
Because a friend to the end
Is a friend
Worth keeping

Beauty of Friendship

Long drives
High fives
Fine dines
Cheap buys
Amazing laughs
Photographs
Honesty
Memories

True

A true friend loves you
Completely
Openly
And
Honestly
They strive for the best in you
And everything you do
They will pick you up when you fall down
And will turn a frown into a smile
They will protect you
Because that is what true, friends do

F.R.I.E.N.D.S.

Let me spell it out for
Faithful
Reassuring
Important
Empathic
Nice
Discerning
Sincere

*You're the greatest friend
I could ever ask for*

POLITICS

The world is ending, our government is corrupt, society is messed up, freedoms have been taken away, and that's not all.

Dear People

What has this world come to
Putting brother against brother
And young adults hating their mothers
Calling someone fat or ugly because they don't fit your idea of beauty
Or letting someone rule our American Dream with nothing but cruelty
Being fit into stereotypes because of the color of our skin
When we are so much more within
There is this saying that I know
It goes…"All men are created equal"
Right…
If we were all equal
We would be treated like people
Not animals that should be separated by a wall
Don't you think rights should be given to all
Let the saying *Love Trumps Hate* be spoken from ocean to ocean
Because who are we to judge if we do not truly understand
Why are men held higher than women
Because without women there would be no men
When did the word *No* start to mean *Yes*
Nobody asks to be violated, abused or harmed
If you think so I strongly believe, you are wrong
We need to change the world for the better
And that won't happen if we don't stand together
This message goes out to anyone who wants change
You do not have to agree with what I am saying
Just know for the rest of my life I am praying
For the safety of you all
So stand tall

The Shed of Blood

So much blood has been shed
And everyone is mourning the dead
From the bullets leaving guns
And politicians biting their tongues
With innocent people getting murdered
And slowly more and more bodies keep being discovered
There are too many monsters lurking around
While people are getting kidnapped never to be found
Police brutalities of a young man walking down the street
Because he is not the skin color that they want to see
Rather than talk about the cruelness in the world
The news spends more time on who is the prettiest boy or girl
It seems like we are trying to cover our eyes
From the injustices we wish were lies
But we can't cover up all the blood that has been shed
Because I am not the only one that cares about the dead

We The People

We need to save ourselves
From the matrix of bullshit
That makes us want to
Be silent
Stand still
Not question
But we are the people
Of United States of America
And we will
Raise our voices
Stand tall
Question everything
Because our lives depend on it

The Government

The government
Lies
Cheats
And
Steals
No, wonder why people do not trust it
I do not trust it
Because I do not want to believe another lie

Greatest Generation

Don't hate my generation
We are trying to fix the mistakes
The mistakes of the past generations
The mistakes that hinder our future
We want the world to be better
So let us change it
Because this dumb, social media addicted, annoying generation
Is about to make change

The world is still ending

Mental Health

It's okay to not be okay

Untitled

It's not a joke
It's something real
Something that can kill

1,2,3,4

1 cut
2 cut
3 cut
4
Cut away the pain that hurts me so
1 swallow
2 swallow
3 swallow
4
Swallow away the pain that hurts me so
1 scream
2 scream
3 scream
4
Scream away the pain that hurts me so
1 cry
2 cry
3 cry
4
Cry away the pain that hurts me so
1 pray
2 pray
3 pray
4
Pray away the pain that hurts me so
1 please
2 please
3 please
4
Please, go away this pain that hurts me so

Recipe for coping

This is my recipe for coping
Breathe in and out
Countdown from 10
Workout
Write
Read
Sometimes scream
Cry
Try to eat
Message a friend
Try to sleep
Repeat

Untitled

It gets dark sometimes
But always remember to fight
Even if it's hard
Really hard
To get out of the dark

For You

My friend
My enemy
My sister
My brother
My mother
My father
My uncle
My aunt
My grandmother
My grandfather
My cousin
To the person I do not know
If you are battling any type of mental health
I am here for you

; The symbol of mental health recovery

I AM WOMEN

Oh, you beautiful woman
You are amazing

Pretty Thing

"Only pretty girls get invited to all the parties"
"Only pretty girls get what they want"
"Only pretty girls have all the friends"
Trying to fit in society's idea or norm
Hoping I can survive the storm
Eating less and less
Just so I can fit into a size 0 dress
Putting on a pound of makeup to cover up the scars that makes me beautiful
Biting my tongue, because women speaking their mind is "unconstitutional"
Getting plastic surgery because Barbie is who I should inspire to be
Because pretty hurts
Pretty kills
Pretty deceives
I'm tired of being just a pretty thing
When I deserve to have my rights given back to me
The right to be my definition of a pretty

This poem is dedicated to any women who has been sexually harassed or assaulted

Me Too

Walking down the street
Someone yells that they like what they see
Getting drugs put in my drink
Because they want a piece of me
Stalked by a person I thought was my friend
They weren't my friend in the end
When I say NO I mean NO
While you think I am saying ready, set, go
Getting sexually harassed while at work
Because they say, "You won't get ahead if you don't give me what I want"
Songs glorifying rape
Because it is, the way that women dress that causes them to have rape as their fate
More and more women are scared to speak the truth
Because they say, "it's your fault that it happened to you"
While the truth is, we live in a messed up society
That blames the victim before the predator
That chooses male over female
That sexualize women for the enjoyment of men
This all needs to end
Before we start saying Me Too again

I Am Women

I am my mother
I am my sister
I am my aunt
I am my grandmother
I am my friends who bonded through sisterhood
I am my pregnant neighbor
I am the princess in the fairytale
I am the abused housewife
I am the girl high on life
I am the Queen ruling a nation
I am the girl crying in the shower
I am the supermodel struggling to eat
I am the woman getting an abortion
I am the girl bleeding and cramping from Mother Nature
I am the teenager getting her cherry popped
I am the underpaid actress, engineer, lawyer, director, and doctor
I am the side chick
I am the female directors who have not been recognized for their work
I am the women marching
I am the soon to be mother giving birth
I am the woman being raped in an alley
I am the baby mama raising my child on my own
I am the so-called slut or hoe
I am the teenage girl struggle with depression that no one seems to understand
I am the singer being oversexualized even when they say women singing about sex, drugs, money, and guns is not sellable
I am the preacher's wife
I am the woman trying to make her way in a "mans" world
I am every woman and every woman is me

Girl, Interrupted

This is a message from a girl interrupted
That has seen her world become contorted
A girl that tried and tried to become the idea of perfect
In her life, that was her biggest conflict
A girl who just wanted to be treated fairly
And not just as an object for a men
A girl who wants people to understand that being a feminist does not mean
Believing in the "destruction of men or that women are held higher than men"
But, that believes in equality of the sexist
That wants people to know her voice will be heard
And she will fight for what she believes in
A girl who knows this that change doesn't happen overnight
But change needs to happen
Because women are too beautiful, loving, amazing, and strong
To be still treated so wrong

Untitled

Stop dehumanizing women
We are not
Toys
Prizes
Objects
Money
Meat
Or any property of man
We are human beings

As Queen Beyoncé Giselle Knowles-Carter stated
"Okay ladies now let's get in formation"

RACE

It should not be the color of your skin
It should be what's within

Burden of Being Black

Being taught to never wear a hood on your head while walking down the street
Using chemicals and straightening tools on our hair because an afro doesn't seem professional or neat
Remember slavery is a part of our history
Do not forget black labor was a part of building this country
Each black person is NOT a felon
Not every black person likes chicken and watermelon
Or cornbread, pigs feet, fried fish, the list goes on
Freedom, justice, rights, and equality are things we are still fighting for
Black women are not all angry we are just sick of people treating us so rotten
Eric Garner, Michael Brown, Alton Sterling, Amadou Diallo, Manuel Loggins Jr, Ronald Madison, Kendra James, Sean Bell and many more your deaths will not be forgotten
If you are a lighter shade of black are you considered more beautiful
Not every black person is an athlete
Good days are when you get home safe and did not get shot or die from being in a car, mall, house, or on a street
Big butts, big noses, big attitudes is not the characteristics of me
Little black boy and girl should not be ashamed of the color of their skin
All black people do not look the same
Cannot even call a country our true home, because someone is always saying we don't belong
Know just because a black person does not always agree, do, say, and or act the way black people are "stereotypically" supposed to does not mean they are less black. They are just expressing themselves and are hoping that people won't judge them for the color of their skin any more.

Color My Skin

If we were all, color blind
Would there still be so much hate and racism
I guess that's an answer I'll never know
Because racism is America

F**k Racism

I hate racism
I dislike racism
I cannot stand racism
I resist racism
I loathe racism
I reject racism
I disgust racism
I resent racism
I detest racism
I repel racism
I despise racism
I scorn racism
I revolt racism
My point is
Fuck Racism and everything it stands for

The Great America

We cannot make America Great again
Because America was never great
It was built on the foundations of racism
So to break racism
We have to break America
Then Maybe
We might start heading towards
The Great America

Unapologetically

Be unapologetically
Muslim
Indian
African American
Asian
Native
African
Hispanic
European
Caucasian
Human

*The sad fact is
That it is the color or my skin*

ART

I am Art
She is Art
He is Art
They are Art
We are Art

ARTIST

I am made by the beauty of many artist
Artist that never gave up on their dreams
To make something out of nothing
To bring a little beauty to a world
That has seen so much ugliness
I am an artist
And I am the artist before me

Untitled

Let your kids be artist in any way they desire
Because art is this world's savior
It's a universal language that can never be taken away
It is expressed through life every single day
Because art is what lives inside of each and every one of you
And your art always speaks the truth

Masterpiece

The beauty of art
Is that it can be interpreted in any way
So never, say a piece of artwork is ugly
Because it's a masterpiece in someone else's eyes
So scribble, beat, and rhythm away
And make that masterpiece

I am

I am a poet
I am a musician
I am a painter
I am a printmaker
I am photographer
I am a crafter
I am a cinematographer
I am a drawer
I am a sculpture
I am a director
I am a dancer
I am a jewelry maker
I am a writer
I am an artist

Untitled

Artist are trying,
They are trying to bring beauty to a world
A world full of darkness and hate
A world that needs to know
That it just takes a little
Imagination
To create something
Wonderful

Instead of war
Let's Make Art

FAITH

Have a little faith in something

Faith

You don't have to be religious to have faith
Faith is the moment where you believe
In...
Love
Family
Dreams
Hope
Desires
Space
Adventure
Each other
You

Trust

In God I trust with all my problems
In God and Jesus I trust with all my prayers
In The Bible I trust with providing answers
In me I trust with understanding the answers given
In people, I trust to not judge what I believe
In heaven, I trust to set me free

Gods

God
Yahweh
Zeus
Elohim
Jehovah
Shén
Allah
Buddha
The Brahman
Vishnu
Shiva
Ganesh
….
The list continues

Home

I grew up in a religious household
So no matter how far I go
Religion will always be
Apart of my home

Believe

Never
Judge
Someone
For
What
They
Believe
It's Their Religion Not Yours

Tell me,
What do you believe?

FAMILY

There are so many definitions of family
What is yours?

Issues

I have a real bad case of abandonment issues
That's why I love so hard
Because I'm afraid, you'll leave
And if I love for the both of us
You'll stay
Like I wish, my parents had

Untitled

Family is the people you hold dearest to your heart
The ones that drive you crazy when you are together and apart
The ones that will always be there
But family doesn't have to have shared DNA
It's the people that make you feel whole
And lifts you up so you can stand tall
Who believe in your dreams
Because they believe in you

Untitled

With family
I've had the ups, downs
And the all around
It's something that seems
Lost at times
Ready to be found
Something that's easy to want
But hard to have

Untitled

I call it how I see it
And I see family
As whatever you make it
Family is home
So whoever is your home
Is your family

No Matter

No matter where you go or do
Your family will be a part of you
A part that can never leave
Or disappear
So don't try to run and hide
Because, your family
Whoever it may be
Will always be by your side

Be my family and I'll be yours

LIFE

Are you enjoying your life?
Because you only live once

Fools

We are just young fools
Thinking that for this short while, we are the ideal version of cool
Fools that fall in and out of love
Fools that feel kind of...
Ugly
 Naive
  Idiotic
   Questioning
    Unbalanced
     Eager
Fools that are still learning
Learning the true beauty that is inside
That life is a book where the pages never stop turning
And we will never have a map to be our guide
Fools that follow our hearts before our brains
Fools that never need to explain
What life means to them
And that we are just...
Misinterpreted
 Inspired
  Normal
   Daring
    Flawed
     Unshakeable
      Loved
Fools that know it's okay to be a fool
Because that is what makes us cool
And allows us to live life by our rules

Our Life

This is our life
And we can do whatever feels right
This is when we should be able to make mistakes
And have a moment to take breaks
This is our life
To hold the ones we love tight
And to say what is on our mind
Without having to be defined
This is our life
Where we can always shine bright
Where we try to never grow old
And we always look for the fool's gold
This is our life
To rise to new and bigger heights
And do outrageous things
While learning how to spread our wings
This is our life
To wish upon the moonlight
And to take leaps of faith without even thinking
This will be the start of your new beginning
This is our life
Where we try with all our might
And believe in the unseen
Because we never know what is just a dream
This is our life
Where we need to come together and unite
Show what it is to be free
And live our life with glee
This is our life
To be loud and not quite
To speak without being spoken to
Because nothing is ever to taboo
This is our life
And we know how to put up a fight
Because we are the only ones that can say who we truly are
So let's shoot across the sky like a shooting star

Still Here

I am still here
Fighting for what I believe
Fighting for you and me
Fighting for the lives, we want to live
Because you only get one life
So make that mark
Make the world remember that you were here
That you are still here

The Kids Are Alright

As long as we keep fighting for what we believe
And striving for everyone to succeed
While being the greatest generation the world has ever seen
The kids will be alright
Wait No...
The Kids ARE alright

Untitled

At the end of the day
Nobody has you like you
So love yourself
Love hard and completely
And live your best life

Live YOUR life like there's no TOMORROW

www.ingramcontent.com/pod-product-compliance
Lightning Source LLC
Chambersburg PA
CBHW052336220526
45472CB00001B/456